Idle and Drunken Poems
from
Old China

Translated from Chinese by
Martin Boedicker

Greatest thanks for the editing to
Kate Keller and Dan McGiff

Imprint:
Idle and Drunken Poems
from Old China
Verlag Boedicker
Dr. Martin Bödicker
Zum Schickerhof 18
47877 Willich
Germany
Copyright 2015
Printed by Amazon

Part 1

Idle Poems

– That time is of value, which is not used. –

According to the Chinese world-view, the idle life is the most sophisticated way of life. Only idleness gives us a clear view on the beauties of nature and the cultural achievements of man.

– The hasty is never wise. –

And only by an idle life one attains a look at oneself, which enables one to get to the heart of human existence.

– The one who is wise, understands to go idle through life. –

The idle life as an ideal – many Chinese poets celebrate it. In a most poetic way they explain to us their love of idleness.

Enjoy reading

Martin Boedicker

A Pavilion in the Haze

Summer flowers and the autumn moon
enter into these lines.

Bright days and clear nights
are given me – an idle hermit.

I opened the curtains once
and never closed them again.

Instead I moved my couch,
to sleep facing the mountains.

Yu Xuanji (844 – 869)

In Summer, Living in the Mountains

I moved to this time-honoured place,
where the flowers are blooming everywhere.

Before the hall, my robe hangs on a tree.
I sit by a spring and fill my cup with wine.

From the pavilion a path leads into the bamboo groove.
My silken gowns over stacks of books.

Idle lying in a boat, I sing to the moon
trusting the wind to blow me back.

Yu Xuanji (844 – 869)

In My Thoughts

At leisure, without any duties,
I roam the landscape alone.

The moon shines through the clouds.
A boat clears the anchor and sets the sail.

I play the lute in the Xiaolang temple –
in the Yuliang tower I sing.

The bamboo as an worthy friend
and the rocks as my companions.

Only nightingales and sparrows I appreciate –
gold and silver have no value for me.

With a goblet full of spring wine
I am greeting the moon in the night.

A flagstone walk in clear water.
The hairpin in my hand glistens in the current.

Lying in my bed full of books –
slightly drunk I comb my long hair.

Yu Xuanji (844 – 869)

Drinking Wine

I built my hut amidst this human bustle
and yet I don't hear the noise of horse and cart.

My friend you ask, how this can be?
With an entranced heart, every place is like this.

I pick chrysanthemum from the eastern fence
and watch idly the southern mountains.

By day and by night – the air in the hills is so fresh.
The birds return to their nests.

I know, all this has a deeper meaning,
but I lack the words to explain it.

Tao Yuanming (365 – 427)

Life of a Recluse

Rich and poor are not the same,
but both have a lot of affairs.

I alone, have nothing that bothers me –
loving my life as a recluse.

Fine rain passed by last night.
Has fresh grass already grown?

Sudden dawn at the green mountains.
The twittering sparrows circling above the house.

Sometimes I meet the old Daoist,
or I follow the woodsman into the groove.

I am content,
in spite of my simple life.

Indeed, one can say,
I am far from worldly strife.

Wei Yingwu (737 – 792)

Boating at the West Lake at Night

Reed, reed, everywhere reed
and water without end.

The lotus flower opens at night.
A breeze carries the scent to me.

Slowly, slowly the lights appear,
which belongs to the cloister far away.

I wait, till the moonlight dims a bit,
thus I can see the lake truly glistening.

Su Dongpo (1037 – 1101)

In the Green North

Where the sun disappears behind the western hills,
I am looking for the monk in his hut of straw.

Only fallen leaves I find – where is he?
I go to look for him among the clouds.

Alone he tolls the bell at dusk.
Idly he rests on his cane.

In this world of purity and stillness
I am free of love and hate.

Li Shangyin (813 – 858)

Alone in the Spring Night

In this pleasant landscape
I leave everything worldly behind.

Idly and leisurely
my life passes by.

The evening is clear –
the wind wafts through the bamboo.

In the deep night
the moon becomes my flower.

Between stones and rocks
a spring bubbles up.

Old moss
overgrows the winding path.

Carefree I live
with the lute and wine.

I forget myself –
with the mountain as my home.

Li Shangyin (813 – 858)

Self-abandonment

I sat with some wine
and did not notice the dusk.

Petals without number
fell on me.

Drunken I walked
to the moonlit stream.

The birds all left
and people were not there.

Li Bai (701 – 762)

To Dan Qiu, in the Mountains

My friend in the eastern mountains,
he loves the beauty of valleys and hills.

In spring he lies in the woods.
Although it's lunch time, he doesn't get up.

A breeze sweeps through his coat.
The pebbly brook cleans his heart and ears.

I envy you, who is without fuss and worries,
idle under a blue sky and white clouds.

Li Bai (701 – 762)

Alone Looking at the Mountain

The birds are all gone.
A single cloud drifts idly by.

We two are never tired of looking at each other –
the Jingting-mountain and I.

Li Bai (701 – 762)

A Hot Summer Day in the Mountains

Idly I wave with a white feathered fan.
Lying naked within the green wood.

My robe had to lie long on a rock,
before a cool breeze blows through the pines.

Li Bai (701 – 762)

A Morning in Spring

I slept so well till late morning –
the birds singing for a long time.

At night I heard wind and rain.
How many petals are swept to the ground?

Meng Haoran (689 – 740)

On the Fifth Day of Spring

On the fifth day of spring
the season's gracious become visible.

The sun shines already longer
and the grey clouds slowly disappear.

The last icicles breaking into glittering splinters
and the first sprouts reveal their red.

Everything shows their best –
it is not only me who loves the spring.

So nice to welcome the flowers in the garden
and enjoy the warmth in front of the house.

Yet still in my heart lingers one regret –
soon I shall part from the red glow of my stove.

Bai Juyi (772 – 846)

On My Mind

Don't grieve for the past.
It only awakens pain and sorrow.

Don't think of the future.
It only makes you sad and blue.

Better sit at day thoughtless in your chair
and sink by night listless into your bed.

When food comes – open your mouth.
When sleep comes – close your eyes.

Bai Juyi (772 – 846)

My Servant Announces the Dawn

My servant announces the dawn
and asks, if I do not want to get up.

But it is cold so early morning.
One should better not leave the house.

Guests will not come today.
What shall I do with the idle hours?

There, where a faint sunshine falls,
I will enjoy my wine and open a book.

Bai Juyi (772 – 846)

Sleeping on Horseback

We had rode long,
but the inn is still far away.

I am so tired, I close my eyes
and for a moment I fall asleep.

The whip still dangles under my arm.
In my left hand the reins are hanging.

Startled I turn to question my servant.
"We have not even made a hundred paces." he said.

Body and mind were separate for a short time.
Swift and slow had exchanged their place.

This short span on the back of my horse
was endlessly long in my dreams.

True indeed are the words of the wise man:
"Hundred years are but a moment of sleep."

Bai Juyi (772 – 846)

22

Idle Life

He, who's heart lacks nothing,
is rich.

He, who has time and leisure,
is noble.

Are you noble and rich,
why striving for a high position.

Bai Juyi (772 – 846)

The Song of Laziness

I could get patronage,
but I am too lazy to ask for it.

I have got land,
but I am too lazy to farm it.

My house leaks,
but I am too lazy to repair it.

My clothes have holes,
but I am too lazy to darn them.

I have wine,
but I am too lazy to fill my cup.

So it's just the same
as if the bottle would be empty.

I have a lute,
but I am too lazy to play.

So it's just the same
as if it had no strings.

My wife tells me,
we have no bread.

I would bake,
but I am too lazy to grind.

My relatives and friends
write me letters.

I would like to read them,
but I am too lazy to open them.

I have always been told that Ji Shuye
passed his live in greatest idleness.

But he played the harp and forged metal.
So even he was not as lazy as I am.

Bai Juyi (772 – 846)

Bamboo Lodge

Alone I sit in a bamboo grove,
playing the lute and sing to my heart's content.

Deep in the forest — who know's I am here?
It is the bright moon who comes to shine on me.

Wang Wei (699 – 759)

At Parting

We dismounted from the horses to drink some wine.
I asked: "Where are you heading?"

He answered: "I'm gloomy and do not know yet.
May be retiring in the southern mountains."

I ask no more questions and let him leave –
where he goes the clouds pass endlessly.

Wang Wei (699 – 759)

Seclusion in the Southern Mountains

Since the middle of my life,
I am fond of following the dao.

Now old, I retreat
to the southern mountains.

The good spirit comes,
when I walk alone.

The best is,
nobody knows.

Into the hills I hike,
up where the spring emerges.

Sitting on the ground,
watching the clouds flowing by.

By chance
I meet the old man of the woods.

As we talk and laugh
nobody wants to go home.

Wang Wei (699 – 759)

Summer

My boat is idly drifting
in a sea of lotus bloom.

Lost in this beauty
I forget to go home.

My family knows as usual
where I am.

Because from time to time
some ducks surprised by me take off.

Fan Chengda (1126 – 1193)

I Get up at Midnight and Look at the Moon above the West Park

Half asleep I hear dew drops falling.
I open the door and look at the west park.

The cold moon high above the hilltops in the east.
The bamboo rustles softly in the wind.

From afar I hear the bubbling of a spring in the rocks.
Now and then the birds are chirping in the hills.

I lean on a post and wait for the morning.
Completely alone – words would just disturb.

Liu Zongyuan (773 – 819)

Song of the Lazy Student

Spring time
is not good to study.

The heat of the summer
is eating one up.

With autumn
comes the winter.

Pack up your books –
for the next year.

Unknown author

Part 2

Drunken Poems

Dear Reader,

many of the ancient Chinese poets had a deep friendship with wine. Whether alone or in company, they drunk wine happily, enjoyed it often and plentifully. In the Tang Dynasty poet's love for wine was so strong that a group of them even founded the Society of Eight Immortal Drinkers.

The devotion for wine was also expressed over and over again with the brush. Thus, a large number of poems are handed down and the literary value of them ...

...

... at this point I can't go on. The poems truly speak for themselves. They simply do not need any further introduction. Or maybe – they need it – but not in the form of words. What they need is:

Uncork a bottle of wine.
Allow a moment of silence.

The sound of a quiet song.
Beautiful nature around.

And then read and recite –
as loud as possible.

The cups never empty.
Nothing else is needed.

Martin Boedicker

Layered Clouds

Layered clouds – so thick and getting thicker.
Falling rain – drops and more and more drops.

Everywhere the same twilight.
The low lands become a river.

Wine I have – a lot of wine.
Thus I'm drinking idle at the window to the east.

But longingly I think of my friends.
But neither boat nor carriage arrives.

Tao Yuanming (365 – 427)

To Boat on the Dongting-Lake

An autumn night at the lake –
not a wisp of mist above the water.

Wonderful it would be,
a wave could carry us into the sky.

Moonlight I would buy there –
with borrowed money.

Or sail up to the white clouds,
to buy some wine.

Li Bai (701 – 762)

Spending the Night with Friends

To wash off our sorrows of hundreds of years,
we drank numerous cups of wine.

A long night of deep talks.
Even the bright moon couldn't sleep.

Finally, we came down drunken –
the sky as quilts – the earth as pillows.

Li Bai (701 – 762)

Waking from Drunkenness on a Spring Day

Life in this world is but a big dream.
Why struggle? Why toil?

Better be drunken the whole day.
Thus I was lying helplessly in front of my door.

Waking up, I was looking into the courtyard
and heard a bird singing among the flowers.

I asked myself, how was the day?
The oriole twitters it to the spring wind.

Moved by its song I sigh
and fill my cup with wine.

Chanting I wait for the moon to rise.
Already drunken – before my song is over.

Li Bai (701 – 762)

Drinking Alone by Moonlight

Between the flowers, with a pot of wine,
I drink alone – without a friend.

Beckon the moon with my cup, to invite him.
With my shadow, we will make already three.

The moon, alas, is no drinker of wine
and the shadow just creeps about my side.

Yet – the moon, the shadow and I as friends,
we are celebrating a spring festival tonight.

I sing, the moon wanders with me through the night.
I dance, the shadow jumps up and down.

Let us celebrate, as long as we can.
Only total drunkenness shall part us.

Friendship for ever and ever.
And let's meet soon, far behind the stars.

Li Bai (701 – 762)

Mourning for Master Brewer Ji

So master brewer Ji,
now you're in the underworld.

Well, I imagine
you are still brewing the "Old Spring".

But on the terraces of night,
there is no Li Bai.

To whom, I ask myself,
do you sell your wine?

Li Bai (701 – 762)

Drinking on the Dragon Mountain on the Ninth Day of
September

Drinking on the dragon mountain on the ninth day of september.
The yellow flowers laughing at me, dammed as I am.

Dancing drunken under the moon – the last friend
staying with me – watching my hat blown away.

Li Bai (701 – 762)

An Orchid of Fifteen Years

A rainbow at the evening sky.
The fragrance of lilies – flowing by.

Then I saw her, fifteen years old –
her smile so sweet – behind the counter.

The flowers praised her and the men
envy the piece of earth, where her shadow falls.

So peerless her beauty, but alas, what was that?
I had paid for my wine double the price!

Liu Kun (271 – 318)

Rural Drunkenness

Yesterday night on the way
from the drinking bout home.

I fall down –
three, four, five times.

I stroked the wild strawberries
and the green moss.

And asked them, not to be angry,
that I talked so familiar to them.

Lu Tong (790 – 835)

To Myself

Sing, when you win –
retreat, when you loose.

Though you have pain and sorrow
stay calm and still.

With the sunrise comes new wine
and thus you can be drunken early.

Shall the worries of tomorrow
be the worries of tomorrow.

Luo Yin (833 – 910)

Lonely Drunkenness

How to walk through life –
I know this for a very long time.

Without rank and title,
completely unknown.

Nothing is as good
as brewing a lot of wine.

And now and then
to lie down in the bamboo groove.

Wang Ji (585 – 644)

On Passing a Tavern (1)

Today, completely fuddled with drink,
I couldn't nourish my spirit anymore.

But seeing a group of drunkards –
alas, it would be heartless to leave them alone.

Wang Ji (585 – 644)

On Passing a Tavern (2)

Only who drinks, knows about wine.
No one attracts me like it.

Leaning to the oven,
I close my eyes.

The cup in my hand,
even asleep it does not fall.

Wang Ji (585 – 644)

The Pavilion at the Linhu-Lake

On a boat to welcome the guests.
Slowly, slowly we move forward.

Wine, we drink at the pavilion.
Surrounded by lotus, which blooms so magnificently.

Wang Wei (699 – 759)

Drunken Sleep

Amid the autumn rain
the wine is brewed so well.

The cold house –
covered by colourful leaves.

The hermit spends a lot of time asleep.
Only drinking he does more.

Du Mu (803 – 852)

Lonely Drunkenness

Outside the window, wind and snow blow straight.
The oven is fired – the bottle of wine already open.

I feel like a fishing boat in the rain,
which sails laid back on the autumn river.

Du Mu (803 – 852)

The Inn at the River

Lonely I drink the fragrant spring wine
and leave the inn quite drunk.

Who startled the wild geese,
escaping through the clouds above the river?

Du Mu (803 – 852)

Slept in My Clothes

On a beautiful night I sat behind my lamp
and fall asleep in my clothes.

Drunken from wine I lie in my bed –
as often – the wrong way around.

Yuan Zhen (779 – 831)

Asking Mr. Liu

Green-yellow and sparkling is the fresh wine.
Brick-red are the flames in the oven.

It's getting dark and about to snow.
Shall we not share a cup?

Bai Juyi (772 – 846)

Better Come Drink Wine with Me (1)

Don't retreat into the deep mountains.
You'll only come to hate it.

The cold water will ache your teeth
and your face will be bitten by the night frost.

While fishing the wind will blow you away
and at gathering firewood snow will cover the rocks.

Better come drink wine with me
and drop together down merrily, merrily drunk.

Bai Juyi (772 – 846)

Better Come Drink Wine with Me (2)

Don't go off and be a farmer.
You'll only make yourself miserable.

In spring you'll be ploughing the barren soil
and feeding the skinny cows at night.

The government increases the taxes
but seldom in autumn the harvest is rich.

Better come drink wine with me
and be together happily, happily drunk.

Bai Juyi (772 – 846)

Better Come Drink Wine with Me (3)

Don't go to be an official
a high rank just leads to jealousy and hate.

Everyone thinks of himself to be so wise,
but still is struggling for merit and power.

Fish get caught by a bait
and the moth is burnt up in the candle light.

Better come drink wine with me
and sink together down rebelliously, rebelliously drunk.

Bai Juyi (772 – 846)

Better Come Drink Wine with Me (4)

Don't enter the world of commerce.
Soon you will lose your strength.

One fights each other
to get hold of the hair of an ox.

Put out the fire of your greed
and don't hide a knife behind your smile.

Better come drink wine with me
and lie together mellowly, mellowly drunk.

Bai Juyi (772 – 846)

Aboard a Boat at Night, Drinking with My Wife

Above the coast the moon is rising.
The boats casts their shadows.

My wife and I, we are drinking alone –
much better than with guests.

Slowly the moon shines fully.
The darkness vanishes step by step.

Why fetch a candle?
It is so wonderful, as it is!

Mei Yaochen (1002 – 1060)

Written, while Recovering from a Hangover

A small grove
gives me shelter from daylight.

In the fragrance of the incense
I recover from a hangover.

But what,
if the thirst comes back in the evening?

Alas, I hear,
already mussels are sold.

Pi Rixiu (834 – 883)

Printed in Great Britain
by Amazon.co.uk, Ltd.,
Marston Gate.